Original title:
Light of the Void

Copyright © 2024 Swan Charm
All rights reserved.

Author: Aron Pilviste
ISBN HARDBACK: 978-9908-1-2029-4
ISBN PAPERBACK: 978-9908-1-2030-0
ISBN EBOOK: 978-9908-1-2031-7

Twinkling in the Abyss

In the dark where silence clings,
Stars are whispers on the wing.
Each twinkle holds a secret true,
A distant song, a dream anew.

Lost in space, we drift and sway,
Moments dance, then fade away.
Luminous hopes in shadows cast,
A fleeting glance, eternity vast.

Echoes of the night unfold,
Stories written, ancient, bold.
Through the void, their light does race,
In the abyss, we find our place.

Every flicker, every spark,
Guides the wanderers in the dark.
With each breath, a spark ignites,
Illuminating lonely nights.

Yet in this vast, unending sea,
There's a spark of mystery.
Twinkling lights, our hearts connect,
In the unknown, we find respect.

Shards of Luminous Time

Time is scattered like broken glass,
Reflections lost, moments pass.
Each shard glimmers, tells a tale,
Of laughter bright, or a silent wail.

In the corridors of the mind,
Fragments of joy we seek to find.
Chasing echoes through the night,
In the darkness, searching for light.

Whispers linger in the air,
Tales of love and moments rare.
Each piece shines, a vivid hue,
Reminders of what once was true.

Yet time is fleeting, ever wry,
Like distant stars that light the sky.
We gather memories, hold them tight,
Shards of time that spark the night.

In the tapestry of living dreams,
Life's luminescence softly gleams.
Embrace each moment, let it flow,
Shards of time help us to grow.

Aether's Distant Flame

In shadows cast by stars so bright,
A whisper glows, a tale of light.
It dances soft on night's cool breath,
A timeless flicker, defying death.

Across the void where dreams are spun,
A thread of hope, a song begun.
Each heartbeat trails the sparks that roam,
Aether's warmth, our distant home.

In silence deep, where echoes play,
We chase the dawn, we seek the sway.
A flicker here, a glimmer there,
In vast expanse, we lay our prayer.

With every pulse, a story told,
Of brave hearts bold, and spirits gold.
The flame ignites, it lights the cold,
Aether's promise to behold.

And in that light, we find our way,
Through tangled paths, come what may.
A distant flame, forever near,
In its embrace, we cast our fear.

Phantoms of the Luminous Night

The sky awakens with whispers bright,
As shadows dance in silver light.
Ghostly forms sway, delight in view,
Phantoms weave tales, both old and new.

Each star a beacon, soft and bold,
With secrets deep, yet to be told.
They guide our steps through midnight's grace,
In search of moments time can't erase.

A chill runs through the twilight air,
A haunting presence lingers there.
Through silken veils, they gently glide,
In luminous realms, they softly bide.

The night unfurls, its magic shown,
To those who wander, to those alone.
In phantom realms of dreams untold,
The luminous night doth swiftly hold.

Together, we embrace the dark,
With every heartbeat, every spark.
As visions fade and shadows bloom,
We welcome dreams, dispelling gloom.

Dazzle Amidst the Abyss

In depths where silence swells and sways,
A tapestry of stars displays.
With radiant hues, the dark unfolds,
Dazzling stories yet untold.

Beneath the waves of endless night,
A flicker stirs, igniting flight.
Each treasure hidden, yet in plain sight,
Amidst the shadows, bursts of light.

The abyss holds secrets, rich and vast,
But glowing gems from ages past.
We dive into the depths of dreams,
Where nothing is as it first seems.

As cosmic waves, we rise and fall,
A journey bound, we heed the call.
In darkness' arms, we seek to find,
The dazzle that transcends the blind.

From depths of fear to peaks of grace,
We navigate this star-kissed space.
In every heartbeat, we persist,
Dazzling bright amidst the abyss.

Liminality's Gentle Gleam

Between the worlds, where shadows play,
In twilight's glow, we find our stay.
A soft embrace, a fleeting glance,
Liminal whispers, a sacred dance.

Where time stands still, yet flows like streams,
In quivering light, we chase our dreams.
A bridge of hope, where futures blend,
In gentle gleam, our hearts ascend.

As moments linger, the air ignites,
In quiet spaces, we find our sights.
To dance on edges where dawn meets dusk,
Is to unearth the things we trust.

With every breath, we weave the night,
A tapestry of soft delight.
In liminal realms, we roam and soar,
To gather dreams, forevermore.

And as we drift, the world unfolds,
With stories new, and dreams of old.
In every heartbeat, every seam,
We dwell within this gentle gleam.

The Shining Lexicon

Words flow like rivers, clear and deep,
Crafted in silence, secrets to keep.
In the bind of pages, shadows entwine,
A dance of the thoughts, where stars align.

Every whisper echoes through time's wide span,
The tales of the ancients, the voice of man.
In letters of gold, dreams start to gleam,
A tapestry woven from the fabric of dream.

Radiance Within the Silence

In quiet corners where shadows reside,
A flicker of hope, where fears must abide.
The calm holds a power, a soft, gentle force,
That guides the weary, sparking their course.

Melodies linger, hushed yet profound,
In the stillness, pure magic is found.
With every heartbeat, the silence sings,
A reminder of love and the joy it brings.

Illuminated Fragments

Scattered pieces of light in the dark,
Reflecting the journey, igniting a spark.
Each fragment a story, a time, a place,
A glimpse of the universe, wrapped in grace.

Shattered and whole, they shimmer and glow,
In the tapestry of existence, we grow.
With every encounter, the fragments reveal,
The beauty of life in the moments we feel.

Constellations of the Unseen

Stars that don't twinkle in the eye's embrace,
Yet weave through the night, a celestial lace.
Hidden through shadows, their stories alive,
In the hearts of the dreamers, they silently thrive.

Mapping the pathways that lead us anew,
Through the fabric of space, we traverse and queue.
In the vastness above, dreams take their flight,
Guided by constellations, lost in the night.

Echoes of Illuminated Shadows

In the hush of twilight's breath,
Whispers dance on silver seams,
Shadows stretch with fragile grace,
Illuminated by faint dreams.

Footsteps soft on ancient stone,
Every echo tells a tale,
Of the lives that crossed the night,
In a world where phantoms sail.

Light and dark, a tender waltz,
Merging thoughts and swirling fears,
In the silence, sparks ignite,
Where the heart reveals its tears.

Cloaked in mystery's warm embrace,
Beneath the stars, a silent fight,
Every flicker, every sigh,
Holds the promise of the light.

So we gather, souls entwined,
In the echoes of the past,
Searching for the glowing truth,
That in shadows, hope holds fast.

Stars Beneath the Dark

In the canvas of the night,
Stars awaken, soft and bright,
Glimmers strewn like scattered dreams,
In the silence, nothing seems.

Beneath the shroud of moonlit veil,
Galaxies spin and gently sail,
Celestial whispers call to me,
Lost in wide infinity.

Every twinkle, every flare,
Bears a wish that lingers there,
Sparks of hope ignite the soul,
In the depths, we become whole.

Deep in shadows, where we hide,
Flickers of light will not abide,
They remind us of our flight,
Carried forth into the night.

Stars above, a guiding hand,
In the dark, we take our stand,
Together we will dream and soar,
As the universe calls for more.

The Glow of Infinite Emptiness

In the void where silence dwells,
An echo of a thousand spells,
Where the heart learns to let go,
Of everything it thinks it knows.

Shadows stretch like whispers deep,
In this vast and endless sweep,
The glow of space, a gentle touch,
Cradles dreams we clutch so much.

Nothingness, a canvas bare,
Where we find what's truly fair,
Invisible threads weave us tight,
In the glow of sacred night.

Every corner holds a spark,
Illuminating paths so stark,
Moments drift like clouds above,
In the depths, we find our love.

So embrace the empty space,
Let it wrap you in its grace,
For in nothing, we find light,
The glow of infinite delight.

Luminescence in the Gloom

In the shadows, light breaks through,
Casting soft a gentle hue,
Flickers dance like fireflies,
Illuminating darkened skies.

Every heart that feels the night,
Wonders at the hidden light,
In the corners, in the cracks,
Hope emerges, never lacks.

Gloom becomes a tapestry,
Woven with tranquility,
For in darkness, we can see,
Fleeting glimpses of what's free.

Hold the luminescence near,
Let it cast away the fear,
In the stillness, find your way,
Through the night, come break of day.

So let bright shadows be your guide,
In their warmth, you can confide,
For every glimmer holds the promise,
Of tomorrow's sweet, bright solace.

Oracles of Passing Light

Whispers dance upon the breeze,
Flickering thoughts on gentle trees.
Echoes linger, soft and bright,
Guiding souls through fading light.

Visions weave in golden strands,
Secrets told by unseen hands.
Dreams alight on silent nights,
Oracles of passing lights.

Embers glow with silent might,
Carrying tales beyond our sight.
Paths converge where shadows meet,
In the hush, all hearts entreat.

Time unfolds like paper wings,
Unraveling what memory brings.
Moments captured, light's embrace,
Leaving traces we can't replace.

Through the dark, the lanterns sway,
Chasing fears that fade away.
In this realm where spirits play,
Oracles guide us on our way.

The Breath of Darkness

In the stillness, shadows creep,
Guarding secrets that they keep.
Breath of night, so deep and wide,
Whispers where the lost confide.

Veils of silence, thick and bold,
Wrap around the hearts of old.
In this shroud, the truth ignites,
The breath of darkness, hidden sights.

Flickers of a distant star,
Illumine paths of those who are.
Gliding through the moon's soft beam,
In quietude, we dare to dream.

The void hums a gentle tune,
Speaking softly, like a rune.
In the dark, new worlds arise,
Beneath the cloak of starry skies.

Embrace the night, let shadows play,
For in their depths, we find our way.
In every breath, a life reborn,
The breath of darkness, hope is sworn.

Stars Amidst the Shadows

In the twilight, stars emerge,
Amidst the shadows, feelings surge.
Glistening softly, hopes take flight,
Guiding us through the encroaching night.

Fleeting moments, bright and rare,
Filling spaces with whispered prayer.
Each flicker, a tale to tell,
Stars amidst the shadows dwell.

As darkness drapes the weary land,
Reach for light with open hand.
In the gloom, a spark ignites,
Stars illuminate our darkest nights.

Constellations carving paths,
Mapping dreams and aftermaths.
In the silence, brilliance beams,
Stars awaken our hidden dreams.

Beneath the veil where secrets lie,
Light spills forth, a lullaby.
In the grip of night's embrace,
Stars amidst the shadows grace.

Phantoms of Brilliance

In the glow of fading day,
Phantoms of brilliance softly sway.
Echoes of a time once bright,
Lingering in the dimming light.

Chasing threads of broken dreams,
Fleeting wisps, like silver streams.
In the quiet, truths arise,
Phantoms dance beneath the skies.

Visions merge with memories,
In this realm of reveries.
Through the mists, a warmth remains,
Phantoms weave their gentle chains.

Ethereal laughter fills the air,
Carried forth without a care.
In the shadows, they're unseen,
Phantoms of what could have been.

Shining softly, lost yet near,
In our hearts, they reappear.
Crafting tales that never fade,
Phantoms of brilliance serenade.

A Glimpse Through the Dusk

The horizon melts into night,
Stars awaken, shimmers bright.
Whispers of twilight softly call,
As shadows stretch, they start to fall.

Clouds gather, painting the sky,
Brush strokes of violet and sigh.
A chill dances through the breeze,
In this moment, hearts find ease.

Crescent moon hangs, a silent guide,
With every secret it does confide.
Silhouettes of trees stand tall,
Guardians of dreams, an echoing thrall.

Softened light on tranquil streams,
Crickets sing of hidden dreams.
In the dusk, all fears subside,
In this haven, we confide.

So let the twilight lead the way,
To hidden paths where wishes play.
In a glimpse of dusk, we'll stay,
Embraced by night until the day.

Orbs of Obscure Brilliance

In the night, the orbs reside,
Each one holds a story wide.
Flickers dancing, shapes unknown,
In their glow, magic is sewn.

They whisper secrets to the night,
Casting shadows, weaving light.
With every pulse, a tale unfolds,
Wisdom wrapped in brilliance bold.

In laughter, in silence, they beam,
Reflecting the hope of a dream.
Mysterious paths they gently trace,
Drawing lost souls to their grace.

Beneath the veil of midnight's shroud,
They gather thoughts, both soft and loud.
In their depths, a universe spins,
Where the journey of life begins.

So take a moment, breathe them in,
Feel the depth where wonders begin.
Orbs of brilliance, scattered wide,
Guide us on this celestial ride.

The Secret Glow

In the garden, under moonlight,
Petals shimmer, soft and bright.
Hidden aspects, pure delight,
In their glow, we take to flight.

Crystals form on leaves so green,
A tapestry of nature's sheen.
Gentle glimmer, secrets shared,
In this night, we've all prepared.

The world holds mysteries untold,
In shadows deep and stories old.
A loving heart, a tethered thread,
In this light, we forge ahead.

Moments captured, fleeting hours,
Embrace the magic, feel the powers.
Let the glow lead fears away,
In its warmth, we softly sway.

So linger here in softest hues,
Bathe in light, let spirits fuse.
The secret glow, a kindred spark,
Illuminates the deepest dark.

Reflections from the Abyss

Echoes ripple through the deep,
Silent whispers, secrets creep.
A mirrored surface draws the eye,
In the abyss, thoughts never die.

Shadowed depths where dreams take flight,
Histories blend in endless night.
In the calm, we confront our fears,
Time erases all the years.

Glimmers shine from worlds unknown,
The courage found in being alone.
Reflections beckon, pull us near,
In their gaze, we face our fears.

Dancing figures in the mist,
Every moment, a haunting tryst.
What's forgotten in daylight's grasp,
In the abyss, we breathe and clasp.

So dive deep into the flow,
Let the currents guide where we go.
Reflections shape our destinies,
Immerse in truth, find our peace.

Enchanted Dark

In the quiet of midnight's song,
Whispers of secrets linger long.
Stars like diamonds glimmer bright,
In the depths of enchanted night.

The moon weaves spells through the trees,
Carrying tales on the breeze.
Shadows swirl in a graceful dance,
Inviting hearts to take a chance.

A velvet cloak of mystery,
Hides the truths we yearn to see.
Twinkling lights in the vast unknown,
Invite the dreamers, all alone.

Beneath the cloak of twinkling skies,
Magic lurks where the dark heart lies.
Each heartbeat echoes tales untold,
In the realm of night, brave and bold.

With every breath, the silence speaks,
In the dark where the spirit seeks.
Embrace the calm, let thoughts unfurl,
In enchanted dark, come greet the world.

The Solace of Gleaming Shadows

In the corner where the light bends,
Gleaming shadows, silent friends.
They murmur softly with each glance,
In their embrace, the hearts find chance.

Through the cracks where the sunlight spills,
Shadows dance with whimsical thrills.
Painting dreams in shades of gray,
In this solace, we find our way.

The world outside, so loud and vast,
Here in stillness, the moments last.
Glimmers flicker, secrets bloom,
In the warmth of the softening gloom.

Each shadow tells a story true,
In the light, forgotten or new.
Through curves and lines, they sway and weave,
In their comfort, we learn to believe.

Underneath the twilight's glow,
The heart's whispers gently flow.
In the solace where shadows gleam,
We find hope within each dream.

Remnants of the Cosmic Dawn

When the stars began their flight,
The cosmos welcomed morning light.
Whispers of galaxies collide,
In the remnants where dreams abide.

Colors burst in radiant hues,
As the universe sings its muse.
Comets trail across the sea,
Of infinite possibilities.

In the dawn of creation's grace,
Time unveils a vast embrace.
Each flicker of light, a new design,
In the tapestry of the divine.

Echoes of what has come before,
Resound in the cosmic lore.
Wisps of stardust fill the night,
In the remnants shining bright.

As we trace the paths of old,
Dreams unravel, stories unfold.
In the dawn's warm gentle breath,
We find life beyond the death.

The Luminary's Embrace

In the heart of the velvet night,
Shimmers a beacon, pure and bright.
Holding the hopes of weary souls,
In its warmth, the spirit rolls.

The luminary, bold and wise,
Illuminates the darkest skies.
Its glow beckons with gentle grace,
Welcoming all into its space.

Through the shadows, it softly glides,
Carving pathways where truth abides.
In every flicker, every beam,
Lies the promise of a dream.

With arms stretched wide, it pulls us near,
Banishes doubt, dispels the fear.
In the embrace of light divine,
Hearts awaken, souls align.

As dawn approaches, the glow remains,
Kissing the world with hopeful strains.
In the luminary's bright embrace,
We find our light, we find our place.

Veils of Illusory Radiance

In shadows cast by fading light,
A dance of colors, bold and bright.
Whispers float on gentle breeze,
Secrets held with quiet ease.

They shimmer soft, a fleeting grace,
A tapestry we can't erase.
Reality bends in their sway,
While dreams and truth silently play.

Through layers thick, the truth may hide,
Yet hope emerges, a guiding tide.
In every glance, a story spun,
Veils dissolve with the morning sun.

A canvas vast, the mind's delight,
Illusions fade with radiant flight.
A journey starts with each new day,
In veils of light, we find our way.

Sunbeams in the Eclipse

Darkness cloaks the blazing sphere,
Yet sunbeams pierce, their warmth draws near.
A cosmic dance, both fierce and grand,
Time stands still, our hearts expand.

In shadows deep, a glimmer's cast,
Moments fleeting, but meant to last.
Where light and dark collide and blend,
We seek the truth that knows no end.

The whispers of an age-old tale,
Of hope reborn when spirits sail.
Like sunbeams tracing nature's art,
They breathe a light that lifts the heart.

In brief embrace, we find our peace,
A love that whispers, "Never cease."
Through fleeting days, our paths entwine,
In sunbeams' glow, our spirits shine.

The Embrace of Ethereal Glow

As twilight wraps the world in grace,
An ethereal touch, a soft embrace.
In twilight's arms, we dream and sigh,
Floating on clouds, we learn to fly.

With every breath, the magic swells,
In glow of night, our heartbeats tell.
A dance of stars, a symphony,
The universe sings in harmony.

Glimmers spark in the still of night,
Whispering tales of love and light.
In silence deep, our souls connect,
An ethereal bond we can't neglect.

With every heartbeat, we are bound,
In this glow, true solace found.
The beauty lies in shadows cast,
An embrace that holds, forever fast.

Aurora Within the Chasm

In depths unseen, a light awakes,
An aurora shines, the darkness shakes.
Colors dance on the edge of night,
Guiding souls with gentle light.

Through chasms deep, the journey's raw,
Yet whispers echo, a timeless law.
Where hope ignites and dreams expand,
The heartless void becomes so grand.

With every pulse, the shadows part,
The aurora paints upon the heart.
In vibrant hues, a new dawn breaks,
In every breath, the spirit wakes.

Let us wander where lights entwine,
In thoughtful silence, souls align.
For in the chasm's darkest edge,
Lies an aurora, a sacred pledge.

Whispered Illumination

In shadows deep, a flicker glows,
A hush of light, where mystery flows.
The heart beats soft, in quiet grace,
Each whispered thought, a warm embrace.

Through tangled dreams, the glimmers dance,
Unseen currents, a fleeting chance.
A fragile hope, like morning dew,
Awakens souls, to find what's true.

In twilight's grasp, the moments weave,
A tapestry, our hearts believe.
With every breath, a secret shared,
In whispered tones, the world is bared.

As stars align, the night reveals,
The tender touch that time conceals.
Each fleeting glance, a story spun,
A light ignites, life has begun.

So hold this spark, let shadows fade,
In whispered illumination, be unafraid.
With every glint, the heart will soar,
In gentle light, forevermore.

Radiance from the Abyss

From depths unknown, a beacon calls,
Echoing through the ancient halls.
A shimmering hue beneath the waves,
The light that lifts, the soul that saves.

In darkness thick, the shadows cling,
Yet through the void, a bright bell rings.
Waves of color, fierce and bold,
A tale of courage, yet untold.

As whispers rise from ocean floor,
The heart aligns, yearning for more.
Each undertow, a lesson learned,
In every struggle, a fire burned.

The abyss holds secrets, deep and vast,
Yet from its depths, we find our past.
With every pulse, the night gives way,
To morning's light, a brand new day.

So let the radiance guide our way,
In darkest hours, come what may.
From depths we rise, anew, reborn,
Chasing the light, the hopeful dawn.

Glimmers in the Silence

In quiet corners, secrets stir,
As shadows dance, the whispers blur.
A gentle hush, the world at rest,
Brings forth the thoughts, our hearts confess.

With every sigh, a story told,
In silent dreams, the brave and bold.
Glimmers spark, in measured beats,
A symphony where silence greets.

The vast expanse, a muted song,
Where echoes linger, time prolongs.
In stillness found, the truth appears,
A fragile light that calms our fears.

As moonlight spills on quiet streams,
We chase the glimmers of our dreams.
In sacred space, we find our place,
Connected souls, through time and space.

So listen close, let silence speak,
In subtle tones, the strong, the weak.
For in the hush, the heart can find,
The glimmers left by love, unlined.

Shards of Forgotten Dawn

In fragmented light, the day breaks free,
Each shard of hope, a memory.
The past awakens, soft and warm,
As shadows lift, a new form.

In every crack, a story gleams,
Of lost tomorrows, and fading dreams.
Yet from the ruins, blossoms sprout,
A testament, what life's about.

Through morning mist, the echoes play,
Shards of dawn, in disarray.
A kaleidoscope of lessons learned,
In every twist, a spirit burned.

So gather close, the scattered light,
Let every piece bring forth delight.
In fragments found, the whole will rise,
A symphony beneath the skies.

Beyond the hurt, the dawn will shine,
In shards of time, our lives entwine.
With every dawn, we rebuild, renew,
In light reborn, forever true.

Twilight's Luminous Breath

As daylight fades, the colors blend,
Soft whispers rise, as day can't mend.
The horizon glows with shades of grace,
In twilight's calm, I find my place.

Stars awaken, like dreams in flight,
Painting secrets in the night.
Moonlight dances on whispered streams,
Guiding lost and quiet dreams.

A tranquil heart begins to soar,
As shadows stretch upon the shore.
In this embrace, time feels just right,
Capturing souls in the gentle light.

Each moment lingers, soft and sweet,
The world slows down, my pulse repeat.
In twilight's breath, all worries cease,
As night wraps me in a silver fleece.

Dancers in the Dark

In shadows deep, they come alive,
A flickering glow, where spirits thrive.
With nimble steps, they sway and turn,
While candle flames dance, and embers burn.

The night like velvet, rich and bold,
Unfolds their stories, waiting to be told.
Each whisper echoes, soft and clear,
Summoning dreams from the depths, oh dear.

They leap through time, as moments blend,
With every heartbeat, they transcend.
A fleeting glance, a shared embrace,
In this dark space, they find their grace.

With moonlit eyes that brightly gleam,
They weave their fate through every dream.
Their laughter twirls on the evening breeze,
In the dark, they find their ease.

The Pulse of Forgotten Stars

Once bright and bold, now lost in time,
Whispers of light in the cosmic rhyme.
They pulse with stories of love and fate,
In silence, they linger, and wait.

Across the void, where shadows play,
Echoes of glory dance and sway.
Remembered in hearts, they gently glow,
Guiding the lost, wherever they go.

A flicker shines in the endless night,
A spark of hope, a guiding light.
These stars once bright, now faint and far,
Still hold the secrets of who we are.

In dreams we reach for the skies above,
Tracing the paths of those we love.
The pulse of stars, forever bright,
In the fabric of time, an endless flight.

Echoes of Starlight

In the quiet night, the starlight falls,
Wrapping the earth in silken shawls.
Each twinkle carries a tale untold,
A dance of dreams from ages old.

Whispers of warmth from galaxies wide,
Carry the secrets of the cosmic tide.
In every flicker, a promise lingers,
Softly weaving in time's gentle fingers.

As shadows lengthen, the past takes flight,
With echoes of laughter igniting the night.
A tapestry woven with love and loss,
In starlit reflections, we find our gloss.

Beneath this dome, a universe spins,
With echoes of starlight, the journey begins.
In every heart, the light resides,
Illuminating paths where hope abides.

Aurora Beyond the Silence

A dance of lights in the night,
Colors swirl with pure delight.
Whispers of cosmic tales unfold,
In silence, beauty strong and bold.

Stars twinkle in the vast expanse,
Each flicker a celestial dance.
The universe hums a tranquil song,
In harmony, where dreams belong.

Cascades of color wash the sky,
Painting horizons, low and high.
Awakening the dark with cheer,
A gentle presence, ever near.

Beneath this canvas, hearts take flight,
Guided by the ethereal light.
In twilight's glow, fear finds retreat,
As the auroras and silence meet.

With every ripple, hopes arise,
A symphony beneath the skies.
In the stillness, wonder gleams,
An oasis for our wildest dreams.

Dimming Nebulas

In shadows deep where light once played,
Dimming nebulas softly fade.
Veils of dust and whispers cling,
As if the night forgot to sing.

Ghostly hues in twilight's breath,
Speaks of beauty found in death.
Stars retreat with gentle grace,
Leaving echoes in empty space.

Time drifts slow in cosmic dreams,
Reality unravels at the seams.
In the silence, stories weave,
Of life that once dared to believe.

A tapestry of night unfolds,
In hues of gray and tales untold.
Through stillness, wisdom starts to rise,
From secrets hidden in the skies.

Nebulas dim, yet still they shine,
Fading whispers of the divine.
In darkness, hope begins to bloom,
As light returns to fill the room.

Glistening Horizons

Beyond the edge where the sky meets land,
Glistening horizons stretch so grand.
Colors merge in a soft embrace,
Nature's palette, filled with grace.

Waves of amber dance with blue,
A canvas kissed by morning dew.
As daybreak breaks the silent thrall,
Elysium whispers, beckons all.

Mountains loom, their peaks aglow,
In radiant beams, they steal the show.
Every moment, a fleeting glance,
In the open air, we take our chance.

In stillness found beneath the sun,
Life's merry dance has just begun.
With every breath, we celebrate,
The glistening horizons that await.

Chasing visions that rise and fall,
In unity, we heed the call.
Forever wandering through the sights,
Embracing dawn's enchanting lights.

Echoes of the Infinite

In the vastness where stars collide,
Echoes of the infinite abide.
Whispers soft, like a gentle breeze,
Carried far through time's decrees.

Each note of space sings a tune,
Under the watchful, glowing moon.
Gravity's pull, a tender thread,
Binding the living to the dead.

Galaxies twirl in a cosmic waltz,
In rhythm with the universe's pulse.
A dance of light, a tale profound,
In these echoes, love is found.

Seekers wander through the dark,
Chasing shadows, igniting sparks.
In silence deep, truth reveals,
Through echoes, the heart truly feels.

Infinity speaks through distant stars,
Uniting souls, healing scars.
In the cosmos, dreams intertwine,
As we listen to time's design.

Flickers in the Void

In silence deep where shadows creep,
A whisper lingers, secrets to keep.
Stars glimmer faint, a distant call,
In the vastness, we rise and fall.

Echoes dance in the empty space,
Traces of light in a hidden place.
Hearts flutter like leaves in flight,
Flickers of hope in the endless night.

Time drifts slowly, moments collide,
In the dark, our dreams reside.
Chasing visions, we roam and soar,
Finding paths to the evermore.

In the void, we search for signs,
Connecting dots that fate aligns.
Through shadows deep and memories old,
Mysteries of life quietly unfold.

Embers glint with stories untold,
Of journeys vast and hearts so bold.
Each flicker shines, a fleeting spark,
Lighting the way through the eternal dark.

Dreams Across the Dark

In twilight's hush, where silence dwells,
A world awakens, where magic swells.
Dreamers drift on a silver stream,
Exploring realms that whisper dream.

Through shadowed paths, lost hopes ignite,
Traveling far on the wings of night.
Stars, like lanterns, guide the way,
In the depths where wishes play.

A tapestry woven with threads of light,
In every corner, a hidden flight.
Unseen realms touch the heart's embrace,
In dreams we find our sacred space.

To chase the dawn and paint the sky,
With vibrant hues as time drifts by.
In the dusky glow, we seek and find,
The realm where heart and soul entwined.

So let us wander, lost in thought,
Finding the magic that life forgot.
Together we'll weave the night so bright,
In dreams that soar across the dark.

Celestial Remnants

In ancient skies where starlight fades,
Echoes linger in cosmic parades.
Whispers of time in the celestial seas,
Remnants of worlds on a gentle breeze.

Galaxies weave in a dance so grand,
Traces of life on the edge of sand.
Mysterious orbs in a silent waltz,
Carrying tales of the universe's pulse.

From twilight realms, we dare to gaze,
At wonders lost in the cosmic maze.
In the stillness, our dreams ignite,
Guided by the remnants of ancient light.

Stardust whispers in forgotten tales,
Of journeys taken on celestial trails.
In the expanse, we seek our claims,
In the embrace of celestial flames.

Collecting fragments of cosmic grace,
In the tapestry of time and space.
Together we'll chart the way ahead,
Through celestial remnants, forever led.

Celestial Fireflies

In the night sky, where wishes gleam,
Celestial fireflies dance and dream.
Flickering bright in the velvet deep,
Igniting whispers that secrets keep.

Like tiny stars that lost their way,
They twirl and leap in a cosmic ballet.
Guided by moonlight, they sing a tune,
Reminding us of our hearts' commune.

In gardens of night, they find their flight,
Painting the darkness with soft, warm light.
Each spark a story, a wish so grand,
Weaving the magic with delicate hands.

Through the shadows, they twinkle and sway,
Leading us onward, come what may.
In their glow, we find our peace,
In celestial fireflies, our souls release.

As dawn approaches, they fade from sight,
But in our hearts, they'll linger bright.
For every flicker that lights the way,
Holds a promise of a brand new day.

Eclipsed Radiance

In the depth of night, it gleams,
A hidden light that softly beams.
Shadows dance on silver streams,
Whispered secrets drift like dreams.

Beneath a veil, the stars align,
A cosmic maze, a sacred sign.
In silence, ancient tales entwine,
Eclipsed radiance, a bond divine.

Through darkened veils, a flicker glows,
Guided paths where wonder flows.
In the heart, a spark bestows,
The light within, the love that grows.

With gentle hands, the night unfolds,
A tranquil warmth within the cold.
In whispers soft, the past retold,
Eclipsed radiance, a tale of old.

As dawn approaches, shadows fade,
Yet in the dusk, the dreams we've made.
Eclipsed, yet whole, the plans we laid,
In twilight's arms, we find our trade.

Whispering Shadows

In the silence, whispers grow,
Shadows carry tales we know.
Secrets hidden in their flow,
Dancing softly, a silent show.

Moonlight spills on darkened ground,
In echoes, we are closely bound.
In the twilight, mysteries found,
Whispering shadows, their voices sound.

Flickering flames, a gentle breeze,
Carrying whispers through the trees.
Stories linger with such ease,
Casting spells that start to tease.

In the dusk, the quiet sings,
A serenade of secret things.
With every note, the heartstrings cling,
Whispering shadows, the night now brings.

Fading light, the day must rest,
In the shadows, we feel blessed.
Together we'll brave every quest,
Bound by whispers, forever pressed.

Celestial Glow

Up above, the heavens smile,
A tapestry that spans a mile.
Stars entwined in cosmic style,
Each one beckons, pause awhile.

Celestial glow, a guiding spark,
Illuminates the path in dark.
In the quiet, let love embark,
A journey bright, a hopeful arc.

With every twinkle, dreams take flight,
Filling hearts with pure delight.
In the solitude of the night,
Celestial glow, a beacon bright.

Through the void, the whispers call,
Echoes of life, both big and small.
In the embrace of starlit thrall,
Celestial glow, we rise, we fall.

With each dawn, the stars may wane,
But their essence we retain.
In memories that still remain,
Celestial glow, a lasting gain.

As galaxies spin, the universe hums,
In harmony, the cosmos drums.
With every heartbeat, there it comes,
Celestial glow, as love becomes.

Beneath the Starlit Abyss

Beneath the sky, so vast and wide,
In shadows deep, where dreams abide.
Stars above us gently glide,
In the silence, our hearts confide.

Through the night, the universe breathes,
In every twinkle, silence weaves.
Among the whispers, the soul believes,
Beneath the starlit abyss, it cleaves.

Time suspends, as moments freeze,
In cosmic waves, we find our keys.
With every heartbeat, time appease,
Beneath the starlit abyss, such ease.

As galaxies spin in endless curls,
They hold the tales of boys and girls.
In the depths, the mystery unfurls,
Beneath the starlit abyss, our pearls.

In the quiet, the heart shouts loud,
Lost in wonder, we feel proud.
In dreaming spaces, lost in the crowd,
Beneath the starlit abyss, avowed.

As dawn approaches, shadows blend,
Yet in our hearts, the dreams extend.
Together forever, hand in hand,
Beneath the starlit abyss, we stand.

Quicksilver Shadows

In the twilight's tender grasp,
Shadows dance with quicksilver sighs,
Whispers of dreams touch the ground,
Fleeting like the fireflies.

Across the haunted silver grass,
Moonbeams weave a spell of light,
Echoes of laughter float by,
Chasing the remnants of night.

Each moment, a shimmering breath,
Time slips through our silent hands,
We chase what is lost in the mist,
As dusk entwines with the sands.

Beneath the hush of starlit skies,
Where secrets linger, soft and low,
We find our place in the shadows,
A dance of the heart that will flow.

In the dimming glow we gather,
Hearts ignited, spirits spun,
Quicksilver threads bind us together,
As the night bids us to run.

The Ethereal Hearth

In the core of a glowing night,
The hearth flickers with time's embrace,
Breath of warmth, a cocoon tight,
Guiding souls to their sacred place.

Each flame tells tales of the past,
Ghostly figures dance with delight,
Echoes of laughter growing fast,
In the heart of the luminous light.

A whispering breeze strokes the air,
Carrying fragrances of old,
Memory's embrace, tender and rare,
Stories of love that never grow cold.

With every ember, a wish takes flight,
Hope lingers in the soft glow near,
In the warmth of the deepening night,
Ethereal dreams become clear.

Around the hearth, we gather tight,
In this haven where echoes reside,
Through laughter and tears, we ignite,
The magic of togetherness, our pride.

Elysium of the Unseen

In whispers wrapped in twilight's veil,
Elysium calls with a quiet sigh,
Hidden realms where spirit sail,
Beyond the gaze of the waking eye.

Glimmers of worlds in shadows cast,
Luminescent paths of distant dreams,
Where the forgotten finds its last,
In the shimmers of starlit beams.

Beneath the surface, life flows slow,
Threads of fate in a tapestry spun,
In the stillness, all things know,
A dance of shadows, two become one.

Through corridors of mist and light,
The unseen hums a soft refrain,
Echoing secrets rich and bright,
In the heart of night, joy and pain.

Elysium whispers with tender grace,
In spaces between the seen and felt,
The boundless love, our sacred place,
In the unseen, our souls have dwelt.

Through the Veil

Through the veil of dusk we wander,
Silhouettes merge in twilight's fold,
Secrets hidden, hearts grow fonder,
The night ignites with stories told.

Veils of mist curl in the breeze,
Harboring whispers, soft and deep,
Cradled by memories like leaves,
In the shadows, dreams start to seep.

Paths diverge where echoes throng,
Among the trees where spirits play,
In the silence, we find our song,
A melody that will not sway.

Through the veil, we learn to see,
The flicker of truth in the dark,
As the world fades to mystery,
We find courage where once was stark.

Upon the edge of day and night,
Through the veil, our journey's begun,
In the embrace of ethereal light,
We walk together, become as one.

Evocations in the

In shadows deep, whispers sigh,
Where secrets weave and echoes lie.
A dance of thoughts, unseen, unheard,
The night breathes softly, a haunting bird.

Coal-black silence cloaks the way,
Lost paths that linger, fade and sway.
Each memory flickers, dimmed with time,
A distant bell, a chime, a rhyme.

Yet in the gloom, a glimmer glows,
A pulse of life that gently flows.
The heart feels warmer, beats like fire,
Invoking dreams, igniting desire.

Luminous Dreams of the Abyss

Beneath the waves, where secrets hide,
Luminous dreams in currents glide.
The depths reveal a world of grace,
In shadows deep, we find our place.

Waves dance and shimmer, colors blend,
Mysteries linger, time won't end.
Each drop of water, a story spun,
In silent rhythm, all become one.

From darkened depths, a light ascends,
A beacon bright, where hope transcends.
In ocean's heart, we drift and sway,
Luminous dreams guide our way.

Fading in Stardust

Fading echoes of distant light,
Stardust whispers in the night.
Time unwinds, a tale untold,
Glimmers dance as dreams unfold.

Stars weep gently, silver tears,
Embers fading through the years.
Each twinkle holds a wish we made,
In lunar glow, the past won't fade.

Fragments drift on cosmic winds,
Memories lost, where time begins.
In vast expanse, we fade like dew,
What once was bright, now feels so new.

The Enchanted Radiance

In twilight's glow, a spark ignites,
The enchanted radiance alights.
Whispers of magic fill the air,
A world of wonder, dreams laid bare.

Through forest deep and meadows wide,
The light cascades, a hopeful guide.
Each leaf adorned with gleaming dew,
Beneath the sky of endless blue.

Hearts entwined with beams of gold,
Stories of old, forever told.
In every shimmer, love's embrace,
The enchanted radiance finds its place.

Shadows Hold a Flame

In the dark where spirits roam,
Flickering lights call us home.
Secrets stir, they rise and play,
As shadows dance in bright decay.

Voices whisper in the night,
Softly guiding, bringing light.
With every flicker, stories told,
Through the dark, our dreams unfold.

A spark ignites the hidden vast,
Echoes of the ancient past.
In tender glow, fears take flight,
Embracing all within the night.

Through the flickering, we see clear,
Memories held, both far and near.
In shadow's grasp, a flame does burn,
A dance of life, for which we yearn.

With every breath, a bond is made,
In the twilight, our fears fade.
Together now, in flame's embrace,
We find our truth in sacred space.

The Whispering Fire

Caught in the embers' gentle sway,
Fires flicker, guiding the way.
Whispers carried on the breeze,
Secrets unlocked with perfect ease.

Cinders glow like stars in flight,
Painting tales across the night.
Fleeting moments weave and twine,
Beneath the watchful gaze divine.

A crackling voice that calls our name,
Dancing lightly, never tame.
Every flicker, spark, and flare,
Revealing truths we choose to share.

In this warmth, shadows retreat,
As dreams and hopes collide and meet.
Together we explore the fire,
In every heart, a deep desire.

With each flame, a memory spins,
Ties that bind, where love begins.
The whispering fire we embrace,
A timeless bond, a sacred space.

Glowing Remembrance

In twilight's hush, where memories gleam,
We gather threads of faded dreams.
Moments wrapped in silver hue,
Whispers linger, soft and true.

Each glow a tale of love and loss,
In every heart, a tender cross.
We hold each spark, a guiding light,
A haven found in restless night.

The past reflects in glowing grace,
Time's embrace, a warm embrace.
In shadows cast by memory's hand,
Together still, we take a stand.

Lost voices echo in the air,
As glowing embers sing and share.
We honor those who came before,
And light the way forevermore.

Through glowing flames, we find our way,
In remembrance, we choose to stay.
A tapestry of love's refrain,
A glowing warmth amidst the rain.

Essence of the Night Sky

Amidst the stars, where night unfolds,
Dreams are woven, stories told.
The moon bestows its silver light,
A tapestry of soft delight.

Beneath the sky, our hopes take flight,
In essence pure, we find our sight.
Constellations guide our way,
Through cosmic paths, we gently sway.

Whispers of the universe call,
As we rise, we never fall.
In every twinkle, secrets hide,
The essence whispers, soft and wide.

Through depths of night, we seek and find,
A sacred bond that's intertwined.
In starry realms, our spirits soar,
As we embrace the evermore.

In silence deep, we dive within,
The essence of night drawing us in.
Together, we dance, hearts aligned,
In the night sky, our souls entwined.

When Dark Sings of Stars

When night falls and whispers dare,
The silence sings a subtle prayer.
Each twinkle tells a story old,
Of dreams and hopes, in night enfold.

A velvet sky, a blanket deep,
Where cosmic secrets softly sleep.
The stars align in rhythmic dance,
Inviting hearts to take a chance.

Beneath this arch, our spirits soar,
To distant realms, forevermore.
In every glow, a spark of fate,
Guiding us through the hands of fate.

The moon, a lantern bright and new,
Illuminates the path for you.
Through shadows cast, we forge ahead,
With dreams alive, and fears shed.

So let us wander, hand in hand,
With starlit skies as our command.
When darkness falls, it brings a light,
The universe, our endless night.

Luminescent Epiphanies

In quiet moments, truth reveals,
A shimmer in the heart that heals.
Awakening to what's around,
In silence deep, the soul is found.

Each day breaks with a golden hue,
A canvas fresh, inviting you.
To see the light in shadows play,
And dance upon the dawn's ballet.

Whispers echo from within,
Illuminating where we've been.
A journey carved through time and space,
Resplendent thoughts, a warm embrace.

When doubt arises, look above,
For every struggle's born of love.
In sparkling eyes, find clarity,
A world aglow, a galaxy.

So let each moment gently shine,
An epiphany, sweet and divine.
With open hearts, we'll kindle flame,
In luminescent truths, proclaim.

Enigma of the Shining

In the heart of night, a riddle breathes,
A sparkle hidden beneath the leaves.
Each flicker holds a tale profound,
An enigma where light is found.

Shadows play on the canvas bright,
Crafting whispers of pure delight.
A dance of light and dark entwined,
Mysteries of the cosmic kind.

Stars are secrets waiting, still,
A yearning echo, a silent thrill.
What lies beyond the distant gleam?
A haunting question, a waking dream.

Through the veil, the dawn draws near,
The enigma whispers, loud and clear.
In every glint, a truth divine,
A shimmer of hope that will align.

So seek the light where shadows fall,
For in the brilliance, we find all.
In every puzzle, love will show,
The shining path where spirits glow.

Across the Infinity's Edge

Beyond the stars, in twilight's embrace,
Whispers echo in boundless space.
Across the edge where dreams ignite,
An endless journey, a cosmic flight.

With every heartbeat, time stands still,
In the vast unknown, we find our will.
A tapestry woven with stardust bright,
Guiding our souls through the endless night.

Across the infinity's sudden bend,
Where beginnings meet with every end.
The universe hums, a soft refrain,
Calling us forth to dance in the rain.

As comets blaze a trail of fire,
We chase the spark of pure desire.
With galaxies swirling in gentle sway,
We find our home in the Milky Way.

So take my hand, let's boldly roam,
Across the stars, we will find home.
In every heartbeat, we'll persist,
A love that reigns, an endless twist.

The Luminescence of Nothingness

In depths where shadows softly creep,
A void resides, a secret deep.
Whispers of dreams yet to unfold,
In the silence, stories told.

Flickers dance without a trace,
The beauty found in empty space.
Light emerges, a gentle sigh,
In nothingness, we learn to fly.

A canvas bare, the heart can strive,
For in the dark, we learn to thrive.
The stillness sings, a haunting tune,
Beneath the watchful gaze of the moon.

Emergence from the silent sea,
A glimmering path, wild and free.
From void's embrace, new worlds ignite,
In nothingness, we find the light.

So dance with shadows, fearless, bold,
In empty spaces, truths unfold.
A journey born from silence grown,
The luminescence of our own.

Shimmering Silence

Beneath the night, a calm prevails,
As whispers float on gentle gales.
The world stands still, in quiet grace,
Wrapped in time's soft embrace.

Stars gleam bright in velvet skies,
In shimmering silence, the heart replies.
Each twinkle holds a secret dream,
In the hush, we hear the stream.

Echoes dance on moonlit air,
In tender darkness, we lay bare.
Thoughts collide, a serene fight,
In silence, we find our light.

Moments linger, soft and rare,
Embraced by the cosmos, divine care.
In the stillness, we rise and fall,
Shimmering silence, embracing all.

So let your soul in quiet dwell,
Among the stars, where dreams compel.
In the hush, your spirit sings,
In shimmering silence, eternity clings.

Radiant Echoes

In valleys deep where echoes play,
A vibrant song of night and day.
Each note a thread, a tapestry,
Woven tight, like destiny.

Bells resound in twilight's glow,
Whispers carry, soft and slow.
The wind hums tales of yore,
In every echo, legends soar.

Reflections dance on water's face,
In ripples, we find our place.
An endless cycle, truth unfolds,
In every echo, love beholds.

Resonance flows through time and space,
Connecting hearts, a soft embrace.
Through radiant echoes, life shall weave,
The stories held in all we believe.

So listen close, let spirits guide,
In echoes, dreams and hopes reside.
Each heartbeat sings in vibrant glow,
Radiant echoes, let them flow.

Gleams in the Gloom

In shadows' cloak, the secrets hide,
Where darkness dwells, and fears abide.
Yet in the night, soft glimmers spark,
Gleams of hope within the dark.

Through tangled paths, the light will weave,
A gentle touch, a sigh, believe.
In every heart, a flicker glows,
In shadows' dance, resilience grows.

Beneath the weight of heavy skies,
A whisper stirs, a soul replies.
The stars above, they see and know,
That in the gloom, their light will show.

So fear not dark, for light will creep,
In sacred spaces, secrets keep.
From sorrow's depth, joy often blooms,
Like flowers bright in shadowed rooms.

With every breath, let gratitude reign,
For gleams emerge from every pain.
In life's embrace, we learn to soar,
Through gleams in the gloom, forevermore.

Harbinger of the Unknown

In shadows deep, whispers roam,
Carrying tales of a distant home.
Footsteps echo, hearts race fast,
The unknown calls, a shadowed past.

Eyes wide open, secrets unfold,
Dreams are vibrant, stories told.
A path unseen beckons near,
With every heartbeat, a hint of fear.

From silence springs a haunting sound,
Veiled in mystery, forever bound.
What lies ahead, we cannot see,
The harbinger waits, wild and free.

Through fog and time, we navigate,
Time unfolds the hands of fate.
In trembling hands, the truth we hold,
In every heartbeat, the brave and bold.

Embrace the dark, the unseen call,
For in the night, we rise or fall.
With spirits high, we journey on,
Into the dawn, a new day's song.

Beacons of the Hollow

In the hollow, the beacons gleam,
A flicker of hope, a distant dream.
Softly glowing, they light the way,
Guiding lost souls, night and day.

Voices call from the depths below,
Echoes of truths, in whispers flow.
Each beacon shines with an ancient grace,
Carving out paths in shadowed space.

Through swirling mists and tangled trees,
The air is thick with untold pleas.
Yet in the dark, a promise stays,
The beacons burn bright, a guiding blaze.

Every heart feels a gentle tug,
An urge to follow, a life to hug.
For in the light, courage fights,
To chase away the darkest nights.

Together we roam, brave and bold,
In the hollow's embrace, stories told.
With every step, the light grows near,
A testament to hope's sincere cheer.

Flickers of Celestial Despair

In the vast dark, stars flicker dim,
Whispers of sorrow in the cosmic hymn.
A vast expanse, silent and cold,
Echoes of hearts, stories unfold.

Time drips slowly, a heavy sigh,
As galaxies mourn, and comets fly.
Each twinkling light, a tear in space,
Even in beauty, despair finds its place.

Constellations weave tales of woe,
A canvas of loss where memories glow.
Yet through the gloom, a shimmer shines bright,
A flicker of hope in the darkest night.

Through celestial waves, our spirits sway,
In the vastness, we long to stay.
Together we drift, all lost and scared,
In the cosmos' heart, a bond is shared.

With each heartbeat, we journey forth,
Searching for solace, defining worth.
For in despair, we find our truth,
In the flickers of stars, we reclaim our youth.

The Shining Between

In the space where shadows dance,
Lies a glimmer, a fleeting chance.
Caught in moments, not black nor white,
The shining between, both hope and fright.

Echoes linger, soft as a sigh,
In the twilight, dreams learn to fly.
Between the worlds, our hearts expand,
Discovering truths we thought unplanned.

A heartbeat whispers, soft and low,
In the in-betweens, we learn to grow.
Finding light in the hidden seams,
Where life's fabric unravels our dreams.

With every pause, a chance to see,
The beauty lies in what could be.
In the gaps, we find our grace,
The shining between, our sacred space.

So let us wander, explore the hues,
The vibrant shades we often lose.
In the melding of dusk and dawn,
We find our truths, and we carry on.

Lanterns of the Hollow

In the silent woods they glow,
Casting shadows to and fro,
Whispers dance on gentle air,
Secrets linger everywhere.

Hollow echoes call to me,
Softly singing, wild and free,
Each lantern tells a tale of old,
Of broken dreams and hearts of gold.

Beneath the twilight's gentle sway,
Lost souls wander, drift away,
Yet hope ignites the darkest night,
As lanterns lead with tender light.

In shadows deep, they sway and sway,
Guiding hearts that lost their way,
A flicker shines through endless dark,
Awakening the hidden spark.

So with these lanterns, I shall roam,
Through every hollow, find my home,
For in their glow, I see the path,
A bridge to peace and quiet wrath.

Specters of the Galaxy

Stars that shimmer, shadows cast,
Whispers of the years long past,
Through the void, they drift and wait,
Souls entwined with cosmic fate.

Galaxies whisper secrets long,
Echoes of a haunting song,
In the dark, their glimmer bright,
Guide the lost through endless night.

Specters dance on cosmic winds,
Universe where life begins,
In their glow, the stories weave,
Of those who dared, and those who grieve.

Countless worlds in silence turn,
In the dark, a fire burns,
Every flicker holds a dream,
A vision painted in moonbeam.

So I gaze to the skies above,
Embrace the night with longing love,
With specters near, I find my place,
In this vast, enchanting space.

Beacons in the Black

In the void, a glow appears,
Braving darkness, calming fears,
Each beacon shines with steadfast grace,
A light in the vastness of this space.

They pulse like hearts, they throb and beat,
Guiding wanderers on weary feet,
In the black, where shadows creep,
A promise made, a vow to keep.

Beacons of hope, they call us near,
Whispers soft that we can hear,
Through the silence, their light will rain,
A gentle touch to soothe the pain.

In the depths, their fire sings,
Tales of love and ancient things,
Each flicker tells a story deep,
Of secrets held and dreams we keep.

With every step, I find my pace,
Following light, I dare to chase,
These beacons bright, they never fade,
Through darkest nights, I've been remade.

The Glint Beyond the Abyss

In shadows deep, where whispers lie,
A glint appears, a beckoning cry,
Through the void, it dances slow,
Promises made, and dreams to sow.

Beyond the edge, where fears shall dwell,
The light entices, breaking the spell,
Each twinkle shines with fervent care,
A guiding spark in the heavy air.

The abyss holds tales of hidden dread,
Yet glints arise from what's long dead,
In their shimmer lies ancient truth,
Courage found through the eyes of youth.

So I venture where few have trod,
In search of warmth, a glimmering nod,
For the abyss may hide its fears,
But the glint shines bright, to dry our tears.

With each step taken, I feel alive,
Embraced by light, my spirit thrives,
For the glint beyond will lead me through,
To a world reborn, forever new.

Luminous Whispers

In the stillness of twilight's haze,
Whispers dance on the evening breeze,
Flickering thoughts in a soft embrace,
Carried away with the rustling trees.

Moonlight spills like shimmering gold,
Casting shadows, mysterious and deep,
Stories of wonders yet untold,
Secrets held in the silent keep.

Stars awaken, a glittering choir,
Filling the night with a gentle hum,
A spark of dreams ignites the fire,
Under the gaze where the shadows come.

Soft hymns of night begin to play,
Echoing soft through the vast expanse,
Each twinkling star shines its own way,
In the darkness, they weave their dance.

Luminous whispers from worlds afar,
Calling to hearts with their soothing light,
Guiding lost souls like a morning star,
Through the canvas of the endless night.

Fragments of Radiant Night

A tapestry woven in shades of blue,
Fragments of dreams that scatter and gleam,
Each twinkle a memory, old and new,
Night's gentle touch cradles every theme.

The moon, a sentinel high above,
Watches with eyes that know no bounds,
It whispers softly, full of love,
In the silence where mystery surrounds.

Stars flicker like candles in a vast space,
Lighting the paths of the wandering souls,
Each spark a reminder of time and place,
Fragments of beauty that make us whole.

The night air hums with a silent tune,
Carried on wings of the cool night breeze,
A melody born from the silver moon,
And cradled softly among the trees.

In this radiant night, we find our way,
Through fragments of light that guide our heart,
An endless dance where shadows play,
A canvas of dreams where we never part.

Sorrows of the Shattered Spectrum

In the silence, colors bleed away,
Sorrows echo through the empty halls,
Fractured hues in the light's decay,
A spectrum broken as twilight falls.

Once vibrant skies now dimmed and gray,
Reflections lost in a fractured prism,
Each tear a hue that fades to clay,
A symphony lost in a quiet schism.

Shadows whisper tales of despair,
As the light struggles to break free,
A dance of colors, a silent prayer,
For the beauty that once used to be.

With every shadow, a memory clings,
Binding the past with a fragile thread,
In the silence, the heart gently sings,
Of a world where the colors once spread.

Yet hope glimmers in dimmed light's embrace,
A flicker that dares to rise anew,
Searching for solace, a brighter place,
In the sorrows of a shattered view.

Veil of the Celestial Night

A veil drapes softly over dreams,
Covering the world in a gentle sigh,
Wrapped in the hush of midnight's themes,
Where the stars weave tales in the sky.

In the depth of the dark, worlds collide,
Planets whisper secrets ever bright,
Fates entwined as the cosmos glides,
Under the spell of the celestial night.

The moon spills silver across the land,
Casting enchantment on sleeping souls,
Holding the heart with a gentle hand,
As the universe reveals its roles.

Beneath the veil, the unknown calls,
A journey awaits where wonders dwell,
In shadowed corners, the nighttime sprawls,
And time dances slow, weaving its spell.

A celestial night, vast and profound,
Where dreams take flight on the wings of grace,
In the beauty of darkness, hope can be found,
Wrapped in the magic of this sacred space.

The Glimmering Abyss

In depths where shadows softly play,
A whisper calls the night away.
Stars twinkle in the ocean's heart,
A dance of light, a cosmic art.

The waves embrace the moonlit beam,
Each crest a part of nature's dream.
Lost souls seek what lies beneath,
In silence, catch the ocean's breath.

Beneath the surface, secrets gleam,
A world alive, a water's dream.
With every ripple, stories sigh,
In darkness, hopes and wonders lie.

The abyss, a canvas vast and deep,
Where hidden tales in silence sleep.
With gentle hands, the currents sway,
In glimmers bright, they fade away.

The night is young, yet time stands still,
In glimmering depths, we lose our will.
A shimmering path through the dark,
In this abyss, we leave our mark.

Faint Flickers

In the hush of evening's grace,
Faint flickers light the empty space.
A candle's glow, a soothing thread,
Each flicker whispers love once said.

As shadows dance upon the wall,
These tiny lights begin to call.
A memory wrapped in the gleam,
In twilight's hush, we chase a dream.

The stillness holds a gentle flight,
As stars awaken to the night.
Each twinkle tells a tale untold,
In whispered winds, their secrets fold.

Among the stars, our wishes drift,
In the soft glow, we find our gift.
For every spark ignites a hope,
In nighttime's cloak, we learn to cope.

Faint flickers guide our weary hearts,
Each moment shared, the magic starts.
In the quiet, let your fears take flight,
With faint flickers, embrace the night.

The Silent Aurora

In whispers soft, the colors blend,
A silent aurora, time to spend.
With hues that paint the canvas sky,
In gentle light, the spirits fly.

Green and gold in twilight's breath,
The dance of life, the hush of death.
Each wisp of light, a story spun,
In nature's embrace, we are all one.

Beneath the veil of twilight's grace,
We find our home, our sacred place.
As colors swirl and shadows play,
In silent awe, we drift away.

The earth rejoices, the night is still,
The vibrant hues a tender thrill.
In solitude, we feel the pull,
The silent aurora, beautiful.

Awake our dreams in colored streams,
In every heart, a thousand beams.
The silent night, a gift so rare,
In every breath, we feel the air.

Cascades of Ethereal Light

In the forest, where shadows dwell,
Cascades of light weave a magical spell.
Through branches tall and leaves that sigh,
The whispers of nature softly cry.

Golden beams like tears of joy,
As if the sun found a hidden toy.
Each shimmer dances on the ground,
In the cool shade, magic is found.

With every step, the world awakes,
In light's embrace, the heartbeat quakes.
Reflections glimmer in the stream,
A trend of grace, a fleeting dream.

Nature's canvas, wide and bright,
Cascades of ethereal light.
In every corner, wonder plays,
In sunlit mornings and misty days.

Let your spirit roam and soar,
In cascades of light, there's so much more.
So breathe in deep, and close your eyes,
For in this magic, the heart flies.